This
Book
Belongs
To _

Grolier Enterprises Inc.
SHERMAN TURNPIKE, DANBURY, CONNECTICUT 06816

Book Club Edition

An
ALICE
IN
BIBLELAND ®
Storybook

The
STORY
Of
EXODUS

Written by Alice Joyce Davidson
Illustrated by Victoria Marshall

Text copyright © 1989 by Alice Joyce Davidson
Art copyright © 1989 by The C.R. Gibson Company
Published by The C.R. Gibson Company
Norwalk, Connecticut 06856
Printed in the United States of America

A little girl named Alice
Had a Bible storybook.
She often liked to read it
As she sat beside a brook.

One day she picked a story
That was thrilling as can be,
All about a man named Moses
And the parting of a sea.

As Alice read, the airmail bird
Stopped by for just a minute
To deliver her a letter
With this little message in it:

"Reading is the special key
To take you where you want to be."

Her book became a great big screen.
The screen grew tall and wide,
And Alice took a little walk
To Bibleland inside.

She looked around, and suddenly
Much to her surprise,
An Israelite named Moses
Appeared before her eyes.

A cruel Egyptian Pharaoh,
Many years ago,
Had enslaved the Israelites
And became their bitter foe.

Now, God had called on Moses
And gave him this command:
"Free the Israelites from Egypt
And lead them from that land."

So Moses went to the Pharaoh
And made this solemn plea,
"Let God's chosen people go.
Let them all be free."

The Pharaoh answered angrily,
"Let your people go?
Why, who will work and slave for me?
The answer's no, No, NO!"

God chose to send a message
To show His awesome might.
The Nile River flowed with blood
Before that very night.

The Egyptians had no water.
They were thirsty as can be;
But still the Pharaoh wouldn't let
The Israelites go free.

And then God sent another plague
To show His mighty hand.
Frogs of every shape and size
Filled up the Pharaoh's land.

Great big frogs were on his throne,
His table, and his bed.
They jumped and croaked, and hopped until
The Pharaoh finally said,

"Tell God to take away His frogs
And I'll set His people free."
But Pharaoh didn't keep his word
And acted wickedly.

So God sent other plagues to him.
Lice crawled everywhere,
Then flies. . . a million, zillion flies
Came buzzing through the air.

God sent more plagues to Egypt
To show what He could do.
First He took their cattle
And their other livestock, too.

Then God sent more plagues of fire,
And hailstones everywhere.
The Egyptians all got rashes,
Then locusts filled the air.

After every plague God sent,
Moses made his plea,
"Let God's chosen people go.
Let them all go free."

And after every plea he made
Moses always heard,
"Soon I'll free the Israelites."
Then Pharaoh broke his word.

And so God sent His greatest plague
And with His mighty hand
A darkness covered Egypt,
Every corner of the land.

The Israelites all marked their homes
As they were told to do,
So they would be passed over
As an awful plague came through.

The angel Death swept through the land.
And when the plague was done,
Egyptian families everywhere
All mourned their first-born sons.

The angel Death took Pharaoh's son,
And when Moses made his plea,
Pharaoh freed the Israelites—
At last they would be free!

Moses led the Israelites.
The Red Sea lay ahead.
And when they came upon its shore,
Their hearts filled with dread.

For after Pharaoh let them go,
He changed his mind, and then,
He sent his army after them
To make them slaves again.

The Israelites looked at the sea,
Their hearts were filled with fear.
They had no boats to get across,
And Pharaoh's men were near.

Moses lifted up his arms.
God caused the sea to part.
The Israelites crossed safely,
Each with a thankful heart.

The Pharaoh's army followed.
When they were half-way crossed,
God caused the sea to fill again,
And all their lives were lost.

The time had come for Alice
To leave this Bible scene.
She came back home from Bibleland
By walking through her screen.

Alice thought, "I learned a lot
Today in Bibleland,
There is no power great enough
To stop what God has planned.

"And those who follow in His way,
And practice what is right,
Will know they are protected
By His holy, awesome might!"